NOCTUARY

NIALL CAMPBELL

Noctuary

BLOODAXE BOOKS

Copyright © Niall Campbell 2019

ISBN: 978 1 78037 465 9

First published 2019 by
Bloodaxe Books Ltd,
Eastburn,
South Park,
Hexham,
Northumberland NE46 1BS.

www.bloodaxebooks.com

For further information about Bloodaxe titles
please visit our website and join our mailing list
or write to the above address for a catalogue

**ARTS COUNCIL
ENGLAND**

Supported using public funding by

Cover design: Neil Astley & Pamela Robertson-Pearce.

This is a digital reprint of the 2019 Bloodaxe edition.

For Soren

CONTENTS

Midnight

My heart had been repeating *oh heart*, *poor heart*
all evening. And all because I'd held my child,
oh heart, and found that age was in my cup now;

poor heart, it bare knew anything
but the life of a young axeman in the forest,
whistler, tree-feller, swinging with the wind,

where *oh heart*, *poor heart* isn't the heard song,
where there is no cry in the night, no cradling,
no heart grown heavy, heavier, with opening.

First Nights

Young father, is that you at the night drum,
playing soft, as though the birds were easy woken?
It's me. I didn't think there was a listener.

Then why, young father, do you play?
                                          It snows
beyond the window, the whole house sleeps – and, love,
I'm carrying something that is a change.

What do you make, young father, of the lateness,
are you a little drunken with the dark?
Yes, my head swims; I lean this head against
the solid wall, and hum to these new cares.

So, go on, tell what you hope for, young father.
Not sleep – not day, not company – just let
snow fall, light burn, glass shatter, let things slide,
let the new change be unlike the old change.

Thinning Apples

Gone untrimmed, when the yield came down
perhaps I'd think that I was rich –
buckets and basins running over.
But all would be small: small blushed skin

small stiff core – maybe of no use
unless for pickling or stewing
or practising to split them open,
like a clasped book, with just my hands.

Twenty good apples on each good branch;
the pruning shears worked in the leaves
answering no and no again
until they cut away to a handful,

all green, and clinging to their stems;
the wind broke through the tree, and maybe
I left it barer than I should
but this was where the thinning led:

there could have been a greater haul,
and yes, I'm sorry how it sounds
but I wanted something different,
and so this is what I did.

First Illness

Little boy, my little cornstalk boy
shaking though your fever;
little silver coin, my little silver coin
in a pocket full of papers;
little shaking chest, little shaking lantern,
can you hear your father's voice?
I'm frightened but I'm here.
Little life, little breath, little
clockwork car, starting and re-starting;
if the road seems long it's because it is.

Keeping the Poacher's Light

The last house-light on in a village is known as the
Poacher's Light.

SEAN McALVENEY

It seems I have it now – the very last;
the neighbours steadily struck out, the headlights
left the island bridge, but this light brightens

and here I do the rounds, checking the bedrooms
for breath, the doors for their safe fastening,
and find a little of this poacher's dream:

the thousand catchings, traps all snapping shut
at once, the ropes all binding – flavour nights
surveying a tapestry of hooks

and lines, prepared for work – the last light used
to memorise the route, my giving streams,
fish in the nets, the large, far off desires

to be trailed home, bagged or slung from my hip –
Such late-night thoughts are sweet, but I can hear
my infant sleeper calling from their cot

so go to turn his carousel again –
this freed horse galloping the music's grounds,
the world ignored as it runs out, stamp, stamp,

hand-tamed, love-tamed horse – its wedded route
seeming to loop from start to end to start,
and does – but there, too, leading night on night

17

the different, longer course, its springing track
guided by the music and the music of
his breath – damn the unhappy, the heart calls,

I settle to the route in the closed house,
thorn-ground, rose-ground, the even, uneven pass;
this first light dims, another takes its place.

Crusoe, One Year on the Island

I know what I'd say,
asked to decide,
between what the sand
and the wood hut

and the drystone wall
had meant for him:
it wasn't the same life
with a different setting,

strange fruit, strange tree,
the old heart running –
But rather: the world
the same as always

but somehow, there,
his life found changed:
the forest gate opens
the same as a hundred doors

but a new voice calls,
and a new hand guides,
and a new heart strikes
where the old heart stood.

Clapping Game

(where [*] represents a clap of the hands)

The blue [*] night was on the [*][*] hill
and my [*] mind was working strangely
after a [*][*] day of [*][*] games

and then [*] and then [*][*], pouring out
some [*] red wine, and watching [*][*] as
the [*][*] moon took its high position,

above the [*][*] house, seeming like a [*]
stamp of something like [*][*] happiness,
I reached the point where the clapping stopped

and quiet in the house, night in the garden,
I was free to play that different game;
up late with the world, my small life leapt,
I rolled its dice across the writing desk.

All the Doubts of the Late Evening

I started at the furthest point,
telling the road it was a lie,
and on I went. I told the wall,
the kissing gate, the swinging sign,

then told the school it was a lie;
the women and the men that passed
I told; each rock, and word, and door.
And I did not spare my own house.

And then it rained – and I told the rain,
and told the rain that I was cold.

Moth

The night he cried himself into our bed
I couldn't find the roadway back to sleep
so went for water – filling the glass twice,
and felt that midnight thrill of being alive;

I heard the clock in the hall in the bedroom –
and *tick* there he was; *tick*, and there, his mother;
and seeing them I thought about the moth
flown back to lie beside its chrysalis,

both – dreaming and remembering the field
one housed and one flew in: the womb's warm evening:
windless, but with a thousand tailwinds rising;
starless, but with a thousand points of light.

Lyrics

Advice?
I leave you the ambivalence of this:
be tender and be tender
and know the limit of your tenderness

Dusk-fall
the hundred questions of the heart
are settled by the hundred answers
of lemons falling from the applecart

Parenthood,
Let me delineate my roles again
I was the night hour's nightwatchman
I was the daylight's stableman

Fatherhood,
Mainly just the one, thorned regret
the thought that I've wasted my life
by not learning more magic tricks

And here's midnight,
and here's three cellos by three seats,
and here's three dreamers in one boat
carried home on the bed of sleep

Waking with a start,
what dream is this?
Who vased the daffodils
in the drinking glass?

Packhorse

Bring on the bit and curb, the saddle,
the saddlebag; broad animal,
steady it goes for its own name
being whispered in its ear;

bring on the blankets, the slumped pack,
lovingly; weight on weight, what matters
is this whole life being dedicated,
haunch and hoof and back; bring on

the tiny passenger, the load-bags
filled with riot; oh mid-life's beast,
it stamps, up the hill of the soul
down the thrilled valley to the stream.

The Address

The village was still there,
its gossip well, the roaming animals
disturbing the street-freed hens,
a place to speak over by the market
where some rope-dancer had set up.
It wouldn't go as I had hoped.
Such a grand evening, the darkness
temporarily violet in the treeline,
I'd wandered back after so long
rehearsing something of the same subject:
the sailor lost to the night's ocean,
though truthfully, I wasn't sure
what the image was getting at
but I was there and wanted to be useful,
even if only to say:
sailor, this sadness or whatever else,
be alive to it, row or don't row,
the hand can pull the fabric of the sea,
there's beauty even in this trauma
and then a few thoughts on living –
no great shakes, I know,
but there you have it – a communion,
since this is what I longed for,
distant, displaced as it was.
Only, as I was making to start,
having shooed some hens to the sidelines,
a small group came up
wanting to know exactly who I stood for,
only I didn't stand for anyone –
what can I say, a voice in a room,

or rather a voice in the open air,
if anything I stood for nothing
but a desire to be there, present in the world;
or stood there just as someone
who wanted to talk, to lay things out
beside the fruit stalls selling grapes
and in my own way to be thoughtful.
They didn't like the sound of this,
and wanted to know, instead,
what apologies I would be making,
since this was the done thing now –
I had none, *I am not sorry*
for this or for any hundred things
if only because I think that life
is complicated and long –
I am not sorry, an accepting prayer,
the sound of water breaking in the stream –
this wasn't what I came to say
but how could I apologise
when difficult and joyed and strange
I wouldn't change the road one stone.
It ended as you can imagine –
me leaving the way I came in
shrugging from the very heart of me,
going back to addressing the other
larger, smaller audience of the evening,
and here is what I said.

Poacher

It's not the pelts and meat I love,
the rabbit furs – their tails' soft fires –
and I don't think I'm drawn to violence
seen here as a knife and a gun barrel;

though yes, there is a second violence
that maybe does appeal to me:
beneath the mud and the night marching,
there's the ownership of things

and someone standing where they shouldn't,
filling a bag that shouldn't be filled;
hand in the sky, hand in the stream,
I hope they take everything they can.

A New Father Thinks About Those Running Home

All told, there wasn't much I understood
about this need to run. The first steps on
the pavement like a knocking at a wall –

then the ears tuning out so that the rest
is just a silent picture show: the drivers
with their last deliveries gliding cages

to the light of shop doors. The night race,
the dark streets humdrum and beautiful.
I had a dream of running, this was it:

long straights, long hills – until a friend described
how if there's a true art to any of it
it happens on the route home, when the streetlamps

are all giving-in above his head –
then, the good runner is just a heart doing
what it's told – *beat, just beat* – and a pair of lungs

trusting they are on fire for the right goal.
Here, up since early, comforting my child,
I have not run – but long to be the runner

if only to gift myself those same commands.
I am so tired, so tired, so young – *Heart, keep on;*
the air's so still – *Lungs, burn hard, burn long.*

Dear,

Still, the shared couch – and, still, the glowing lamp,
the romance of fresh oranges at midnight

The Night Watch

It's 1 a.m. and someone's knocking
at sleep's old, battered door – and who
could it be but this boy I love,
calling for me to come out, into
the buckthorn field of being awake –

and so I go, finding him there
no longer talking – but now crying
and crying, wanting to be held;
but *shhh*, what did you want to show
that couldn't wait until the morning?

Was it the moon – because I see it:
the first good bead on a one-bead string;
was it the quiet – because I owned it,
once – but found I wanted more.

The Disembarked

It's midnight and I'm dismantling a railway,
bend by bend, straight by straight. The passengers
who shuttled all throughout the provinces
of imagined lavender and imagined wheat,
must find a place to settle for the night,

and don't I have a certain sympathy
with those come blinking from the carriages
with nowhere to lay out – except this bed
beneath the sliding blue stars of the evening
near the warm, creaking sleepers of the heart.

Go There

The trick's to go just where is needed:
the baker for the tearing bread,
the forest for its shade; I'll travel
for hours to Uist for the breeze
I know is there.
              Wanting to know
how sore the world is, thrown and sore,
go stop with them – but want to know
what's good, come here; let me tell you
the brief long happiness I've known.

The Water Carrier

I want to be the worst of this profession,
the one who makes it home half-empty, tipping
more air than water from the ringing pot,
and so late back the town's already dark;

Oh no, they'll say, *that's not the way of it*,
and I'll know their heaven's brimful and undrunk,
their lips parched.
                    What do they know of the kiss
on the shoulder of that first spilt drop,

the tuneful *drip, drip, drip* on the stone path?
Midway home, midway from the source, my dream-sun
bleaching the sky, what could be better than
dry road ahead, my flooded road behind?

Returning to Work

I seemed to always be en route
wheeling through the world's traffic, or
journeying towards parenthood
housed at his nursery's wide gate;

on the top deck, I missed the time
the only work was the heart's work,
a tailor in their studio
lost to their full-day occupation

fashioning for the one person,
mending for warmth, mending for comfort,
the needle swimming its new thread;
novice to it, it hardly mattered,

I held the two seams of the day;
even now, walking in the cold,
I think how I did it, and pull close
the [*][*], buttoned coat I'd made.

Measuring Heat Loss in the Arctic

When our strange camera unfolded
the red coal hissing in the snow
as just a thing of decreasing brightness
on an otherwise dark screen

we understood our one concern
was not the cold – but light. Just light.
It was a peaceful sort of work
to watch as things went dimming out:

the flare of coal, the glint-boiled water,
the man or woman who had stripped
right there to nothing – or, as shown,
right down to standing light. Forgetting

about the loss, we watched it shake –
still something of a man, still something
of a woman, but also something of
a burning tree, up right and blazing,

or there, in its bared narrowness,
strange and persistent, stood alone,
something of the glass between the curtains
when it is bright, but late, but bright.

Dream

I heard him crying in his sleep,
my two-month-old – and marvelled, when,
perhaps, I should have woken him;

young, young boy: already he seemed
to be drawing from his human well,
sipping the taste, learning the balance

that must be paid for his new hours:
son, it was always to be the case.
Who'd have known we'd know this so early?

I did not wake him, though he cried,
but bent above his cot – and talked
him through his dream until he settled.

Blackberries

Growing up it was natural to see
those capsized houses,
      roofs yawned in around
the ceiling beams and slate, the heavy door
slipped down and bolted shut against the landscape,

but let no one tell you it wasn't good
running the too-green carpet, moss on rocks,
and chasing through the rooms, our rabble group
wildly there, setting house in the collapse,

stretching out on the floorboards, we admired
our private skyline ripening through the roofspace.
Things fell apart, still it was good. We ate
the fresh blackberries we found in the hearth.

Poetry When Working

I left for work at six
I scoured the forest for kindling sticks

And knew the office till nine
and took my lantern to the silver mine

Too often the work went late
I fished where the river disturbed the lake

An Island Vigil

> ... some held that the sweetness or rankness of
> putrefaction gave more insight into a person's true
> character than hearsay or anecdotal evidence...
>
> D. SIMMONS
> *Folklore in Pre-Revolutionary Russia* (1941)

It wasn't warmth rising from her skin
then, but the smell of weed and buttermilk;

and hers a life of lamp-oil and old honey
her small hands gifted over this double scent;

and there was beach sand and beach salt,
the fruit she ran beneath cold water.

Some prayed. A candle was lit – then blown,
and all that was in the air was smoke.

The Cut

I had gone walking in the forest – not
for any need of wood or kindling
but rather just to feel across the shoulders
the full weight of the question of the axe;

the forest sounded to a hundred axemen,
a hundred axewomen's blows – they never tired,
it seemed, and their trees – so thick – didn't split
or fall, at least not to my listening.

At times, I allowed myself the thought of felling:
the metal blade imparting its own catch
of light into the tree's so-tender bole,
my own bright sweat on brow and hands and back;

ah bliss, I thought, and I swung dedicated,
loud, against the bark of this dreamed tree
or that. These thoughts made the route home seem short,
and once or twice I even stopped to tap

against the length of one that stretched or towered.
I pressed a licked thumb to the wood. Perhaps,
soon, I would make to start. Then, as is right,
burn the rest of the trees to the ground.

Four Memories in No Particular Order

The cut peat drying on the bluebells
and folded grass, rain coming down,
as I proposed by the stone bench,
the two of us in the new silence
in our child's bedroom, I threw a dice
five times, and each time guessed it right.

Horseshoe Crab

Pre-historic creatures... which have hardly changed
in 250 million years

DAVID ATTENBOROUGH
Life

Oh son, while others
grew delicate,
these carried on,
armoured and silent,

marching in their
unfollowed, unlit
torch procession
to lasting out.

Take pride from your hurt,
when the skin breaks
or the blood runs,
or when the chest

seizes and weakens.
This is the line you're from;
here, take the match,
see how the warmth burns.

Proof

Maybe you've heard
the drummer's test,
their one for fame,
starts with the unpeeling

of the skin or hide
from the drum frame;
and that it ends
with the straight hand

against the tenser air,
and the production
of a sound that
the ears, the lips,

and hands might claim
was the exact same sound
as before –

Living in the City and Dreaming of the Winter Beach

I wanted this – to be so far off,
to leave my wake in the sand's drift;
I wanted this – the dark waves rising
like the peel from a peeling knife;
I wanted this – the wave-found lighthouse
beckoning to the wave-found beach;
I wanted this – to stand apart,
to stand close, and be generous.

Two Poems after Cuevas Lopes

Picking Day

The afternoon had baked the ground
and the owner of the farm
had finally left off proclaiming
this time *speed* and then next time *care*.
The olives glistened in their barrels.

Now was the late point of the day;
here, my co-workers slept and sweated
in the shade of the large, red barn,
the gleam of olives on the blankets,
and tired, I closed my eyes recalling

my child's first months, and how he left
his mark on everything: our house,
our table, our own skin. Already
on the road of the dream, I found
his life's tree, picked it clean again.

Leaving Town

Let me leave with a shrug and go,
taking heart that over by
the wood gate and the waterwheel
there's the piled-up locks and keys

from when the blacksmith left, securing
the air since there is nothing else;
ach and ach well, I head away
but this could serve as fine replacement.

Other Branches

If the world's door closes behind
and death is just one stretching tree,
be a lantern, overpoured with oil;
be sure and strong, strung to the branch
brilliant in your old dream of life

or if death is not like this –
but is a sea, beachless and unlit,
then free your boat to the swell:
not lost, not on course, be bare-poled,
but steered and steering nonetheless.

Be ready, change will come. Be brave,
I know that you'll be good at this.

February Morning

The winter light was still to hit the window,
and all my other selves were still asleep,
when, standing with this child in all our bareness,
I found that I was a ruined bridge, or one
that stood so long half-built and incomplete;

at other times I'd been a swinging gate,
a freed skiff – then his head dropped in the groove
of my neck, true as a keystone, and I fixed:
all stone and good use, two shores with one crossing.
The morning broke, I kissed his head, and stood.

Glasgow

I've been surprised to find the *perfect* in strange
places: there was one time at the bar by the low-
fenced, five-a-side pitches – the drinkers sunning
themselves – and the interruption of two small
boys gesturing from the margins: *buddy, kick us
the ball* – and there it was, a muddied skin, slack
and worn, but still with one game left in it. There
was a jostle at the tables before someone chose
themselves – the long run-up, the kicker played
completely – I watched as the person gave it
everything and the sagged globe stayed still – the
man curling up weeping beside it. That place,
they are cruel there. And beautiful. The wisdom
that if we give then the whole world moves under-
cut just as the ball was cut open so it could be set
with care onto an upright brick. The kicker kicks
himself, lost and lost, twice. Yes, I saw it happen.

Cooling a Meal by the Outside Door

Devotee of, what, if not small actions,
I stir heat – and, this one good life
run away with me, I pair things up:
the moon with this tree, the streaming clouds
with my child's bowl – the small works of love
and this dim porch. The night sky opens
and, here, the meal is cool; the meal
is cool and, here, the night sky opens.

Capture
(after Gillian Allnutt)

Brief gravel bird, going

– gone from the stones,

for a moment the footfall drowns the song,

capture won't come – love will

Tightrope

I'd like to be there for small reasons:
travelling on the tilting wire
when everything falls to quietness
below the ropeline,
                    to cross above
the panic, even if just once –
guided right, and making it
on one-third line and two-thirds air.

Thirties

One night I was sitting by my inner life
and it was such a little fire
and, here and here, the snow was coming down.
Doesn't snowfall make everything so quiet?

So white, the soft drift packed along the wilds.
And maybe I wasn't a young man then:
careful and careful, I stepped into the fire
as I stepped onto the snow, and turned for home.

Language

There was a month, before we complicated it,
when the simple rule went – that everything with a wing
was *bird*: the crow, the sparrow, even the small bat

we saw go wheeling through the near dusk – *bird*, and *bird*
and *bird*; and I felt something of how the word opened
and welcomed this bat into the meaning of it;

bird, though it never sang or perched – *bird*, all the same,
even in its tumbling flight, its reeling panic.
Bird, he forgave it – and the world flew into it.

From the Spanish

Here, let me offer this translation:
Cada loco con su tema –
All parents call their river Discontent

and isn't that so – just children ourselves,
we travel down the water to
the cot, and spend the nights unloading

the brimming crates of oranges,
since this is what love seems like now;
our raft so small, the pier still smaller.

Maybe it comes as a relief
that the translation isn't right,
and *Cada loco con su tema*

actually means – *A parent writes*
their name twice – first on a partner's flank,
hip-bone to neck, then, with more care,

(and with a clearer, brighter ink)
along their child, from toe to scalp;
I still remember doing this.

So now, what does it matter if
the translation, again, isn't right
and *Cada loco con su tema*

means *Each madman with their own way*;
and my way travelled past the point
when one truth discounts the rest:

earlier I left his dark bedroom –
but still, it's true, I've never left;
and look, he isn't in my arms,
and yet he's all I'm carrying.

Good Night

No curtains should be open at that time
but ours weren't drawn – and the cold world looked in;
three years into his life, come to the window,
sleep hadn't found my door, again – so up

I watched the morning's morning open out,
the frosted ground, clean as an envelope.
Awake, so tenderly awake, I felt
like the lamplighter of some old city

when the city's lit, and the crowds dispersed:
so much was love, so much was work – I took
the small spark post to post, I cradled it
and let it guide me to my darkling house.
Good morning, here's the brightness in the dawn;
good night, here's love like a faint snowfall. Good night.

ACKNOWLEDGEMENTS

Acknowledgments are due to the editors in the following journals and anthologies in which some of these poems have previously appeared: *Ambit, And Other Poems, Best British Poetry 2015*, ed. Roddy Lumsden (Salt Publishing, 2015), *The Café Review, The Dark Horse, The Interpreter's House, The Manchester Review, Poetry Daily, Poetry London, The Poetry Review, Prac Crit*, and *The Scotsman*. Several of these poems were published in a collection, *First Nights* (Princeton Series of Contemporary Poets, USA, 2016).

I would like to express my gratitude to the Northern Writers Award and to the Edwin Morgan Poetry Award for creating time for these poems to be written.

I would also like to thank the following people for their help and advice when writing and re-drafting this book: Paul Adrian, Alison Angell, Neil Astley, Ian Duhig, Andrew Jamison, Zaffar Kunial and Susan Stewart. And thank you to my wife, Catriona McAra, and to my son.

Niall Campbell was born in 1984 on the island of South Uist, one of the Outer Hebrides of Scotland. He received an Eric Gregory Award in 2011 and an Arvon-Jerwood Mentorship in 2013, and won the Poetry London Competition in 2013. His debut pamphlet, *After the Creel Fleet*, was published by Happenstance Press in 2012. His first book-length collection, *Moontide* (Bloodaxe Books, 2014), won the £20,000 Edwin Morgan Poetry Award, as well as the Saltire First Book of the Year Award; it was also shortlisted for the Forward Prize for Best First Collection, the Fenton Aldeburgh First Collection Prize and the Michael Murphy Memorial Prize, and was a Poetry Book Society Recommendation. *First Nights: poems*, a selection from *Moontide* with additional new poems, was published by Princeton University Press in the US in 2016. His second book-length collection, *Noctuary*, (Bloodaxe Books, 2019), was shortlisted for the 2019 Forward Prize for Best Collection. He lives in Leeds.